THE ART AND POLITICS OF GEOFFREY MOSS

THE ART AND POLITICS OF
GEOFFREY MOSS

With a Foreword by Dan Rather

A **Washington Post** Book

HAWTHORN BOOKS, INC.
Publishers / NEW YORK

Publisher's Note

Geoffrey Moss's illustrations were the first captionless
drawings to be distributed on a nationally syndicated
basis. Subscribers to this service, major newspapers,
receive a number of drawings each month, and their editors may
use his art as they see appropriate.

Of the 111 illustrations that appear in this book, 91 figures were published originally by *Washington Post;* 9
by *Atlantic Monthly;* 4 by *Chronicle of Higher Education;* 4 by *Horizon* and *American Heritage;* 1 by *New
York* magazine; 1 by *New York Times;* and 1 by Doubleday.

For Marion, this is her book as well as mine.

Foreword

My boss at CBS News, Richard S. Salant, reminds me from time to time that there is a company policy prohibiting correspondents from endorsing people and products. It is a necessary and reasonable policy. So, right from the start let me tell you that I am *not* endorsing Geoffrey Moss or his views.

I *am* addicted to his work.

He is a truth-seeker. And a truth-teller, specializing in tough truths.

Somebody once said, "You can know all of the facts and still not know the truth." Every reporter worthy of the name knows and is frustrated by the knowledge of how true that is. That is part of what first attracted me to Moss's work.

I would look at his material in the *Washington Post* and say to myself, "Hey, this guy is terrific. He is *on* to something. Without a word, without so much as a single number, he hammers home truths. Or, on many days in many ways, as close to truths as any scrambling reporter is likely to get—on some stories maybe closer. How does he do that? Especially, how does he manage to do it so consistently?"

So I began following his development, right on through his nomination for a Pulitzer Prize and beyond. I have yet to answer those basic questions about how he does what he does so well, so often. It remains inexplicable to me. But he has been doing it long enough to convince me that he is no shooting star. This man and his talent are going to be around, making a difference about the way Americans think for a long while.

This is not to say Moss is always accurate. He isn't. Who is? The point is that he looks, listens, thinks, then tells you in his own unique way what he has seen and heard and what he thinks about it. Uncompromisingly. He sticks his neck out, takes stands.

Those of us who have chosen to practice the reporting trade in more traditional ways go about what we do differently. We swear by the discipline that says get the facts straight, get the quotes exactly and in context, treat what you get fairly and objectively insofar as that is humanly possible. That remains, as I believe it should, the mainstream of American journalism. Moss is in another stream, one that allows him to engage in outright editorializing and satire.

That is part of the reason why whether one agrees with him or not (I often disagree with what he has to say), he is rarely dull and at the very least makes one *think* about what is happening. And whether one agrees that a particular illustration of his on any given day is hitting on a truth or not, one can usually recognize that he has packed a lot of information into it.

Perhaps that, as much as anything, is what I find so addictive about his work: He is amusing and informative.

— DAN RATHER

Georgetown, Washington, D.C.
February 1, 1977

Preface

The words do not come easy; they never have. Images, instead, thousands and thousands of images, populate my lexicon.

"Isn't it frightening to have them all inside your head all the time?" my wife, Marion, asked in my studio one morning.

I replied easily, confidently, because I'd been awaiting that question for years. "It would be more frightening *not* to have them!"

Their source is the inevitable conflict that results from the fact that more than one organism has chosen to make its home on this particular planet. The machinations are endless: Two parties dispute their rights to a territory; one party fancies itself more capable than another; a leader is embarrassed by congressional findings. They translate themselves, sometimes literally, more often not, into the pictures I draw: a house divided, women's struggle for equality, the plight of a past president. Always there is conflict; sometimes there are apologies, but never sufficient to erase the absurdities that draw themselves each day into the news. And they stand, like yelping paperboys, peddling their wares on the world's street corners.

Because my drawings are usually seen in newspapers and associated with current crises, they have been called political, yet they bear no traditional captions or tags. Here such labels would only prove redundant, for the symbols, I feel, are strong enough to communicate my ideas.

— GEOFFREY MOSS

New York
January 1977

Acknowledgments

Above all, my thanks to Stanley J. Hinden, my first editor at the *Washington Post*, and William Dickinson, director of the Washington Post Writers Group, for their journalistic experience and encouragement.

Recognition of my work would not have been possible without the help of the following people: Kathrine Graham, Benjamin C. Bradlee, Philip Geyelin, Park Teter, Joel Garreau, Eric Seidman, David Gunderson, Debbie Wolfe, Herbert M. Rosenthal, Ira Silberlicht, Tom Lennon, Stan Mack, Terry Brown, Robert Manning, Edward R. Weidlein, and Thomas Hoving.

My particular gratitude goes to my editor, Sandra Choron, who proposed this book, and to Herbert Lubalin, who was the first to publish an article on my collected works.

I wish to extend my appreciation to the following publications for permission to reprint a number of illustrations that appeared originally in their publications: the *Atlantic Monthly*, the *Chronicle of Higher Education*, *Horizon* and *American Heritage*, the *New York Times*, *New York* magazine, and Doubleday (*Agent K13: The Super-Spy*).

I include special thanks to Professor Francis P. Colburn and Lincoln Epworth, for his counsel and friendship over the years, and to my parents and my wife, Marion, for making the sacrifices that allowed me to indulge in my work freely.

THE ART AND POLITICS OF GEOFFREY MOSS

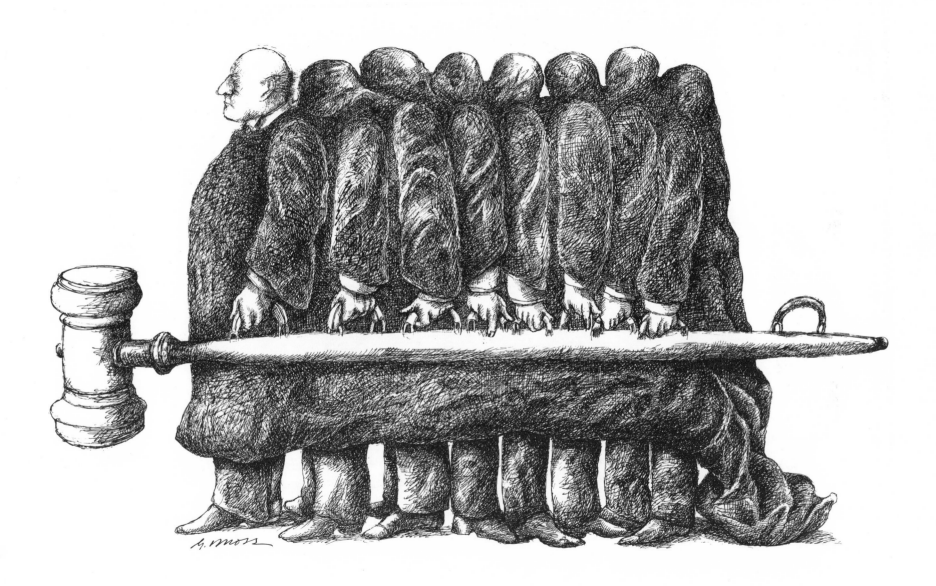

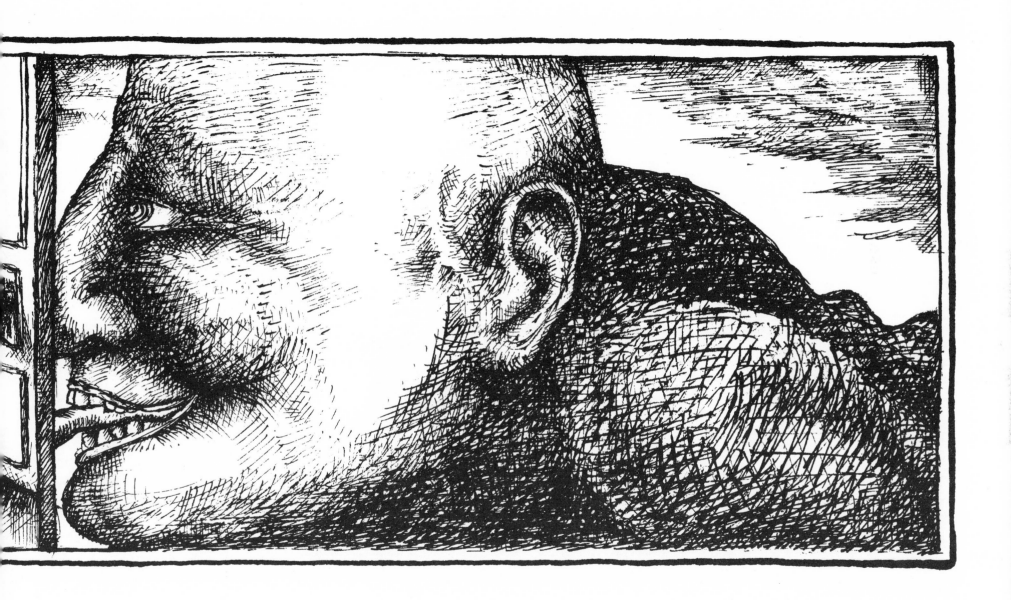

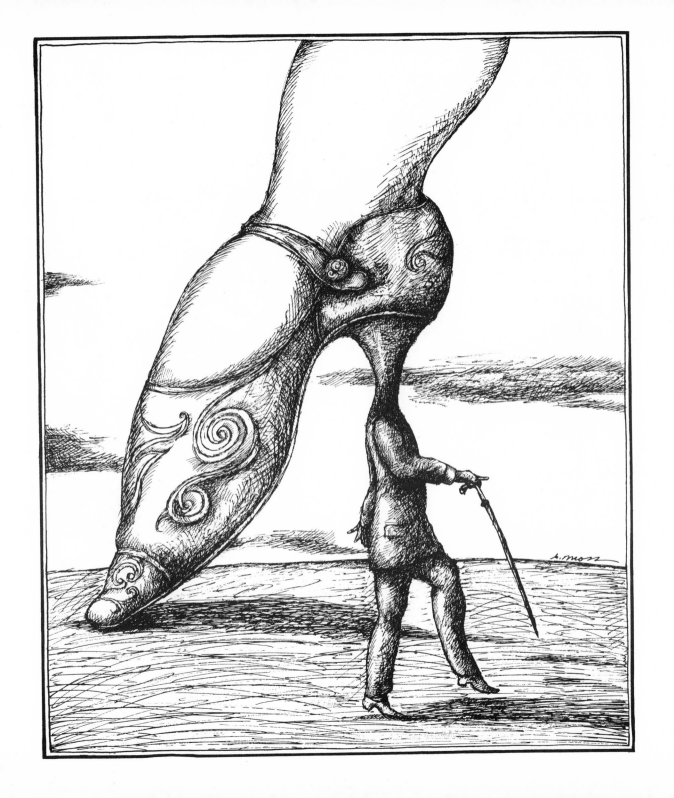

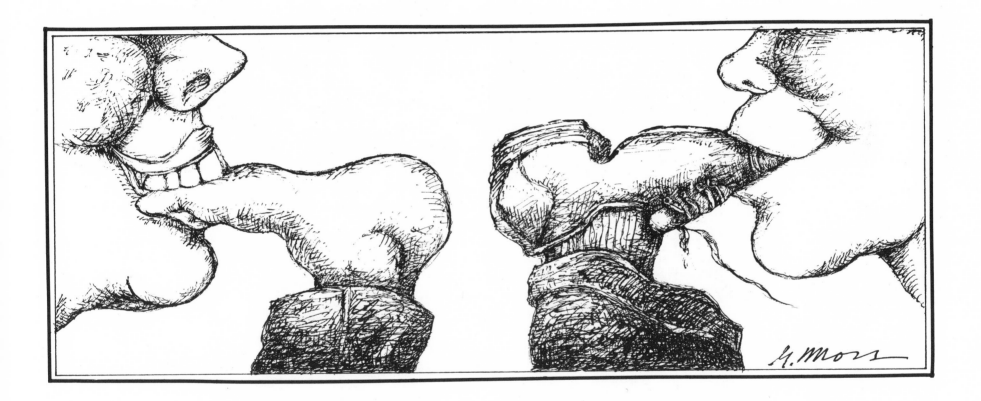

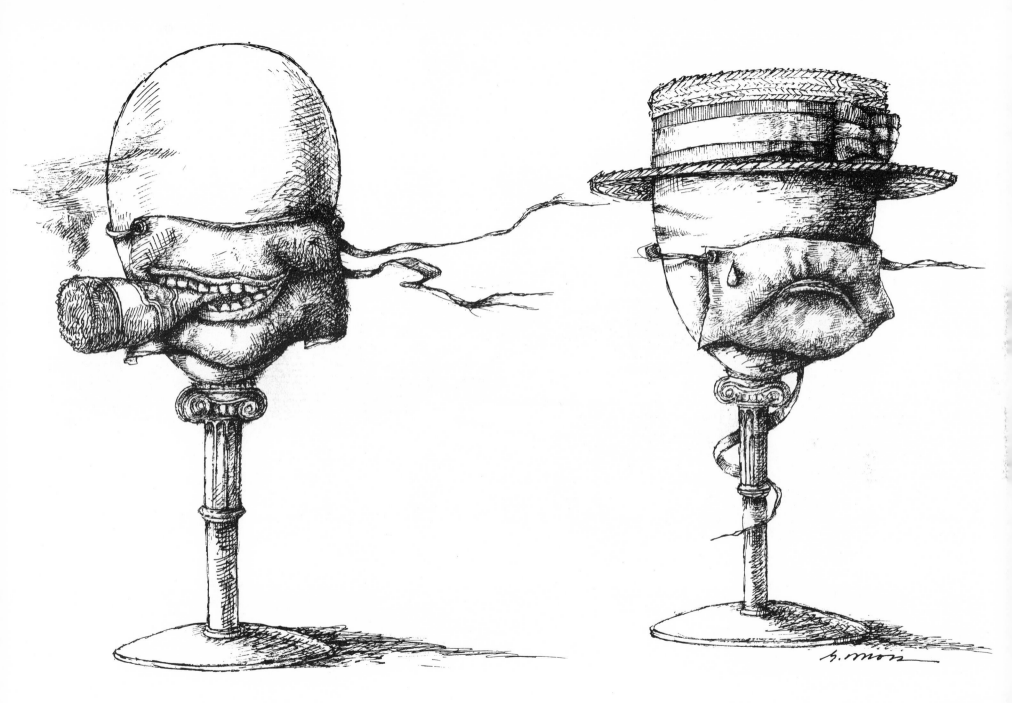

g. moss

g. moss

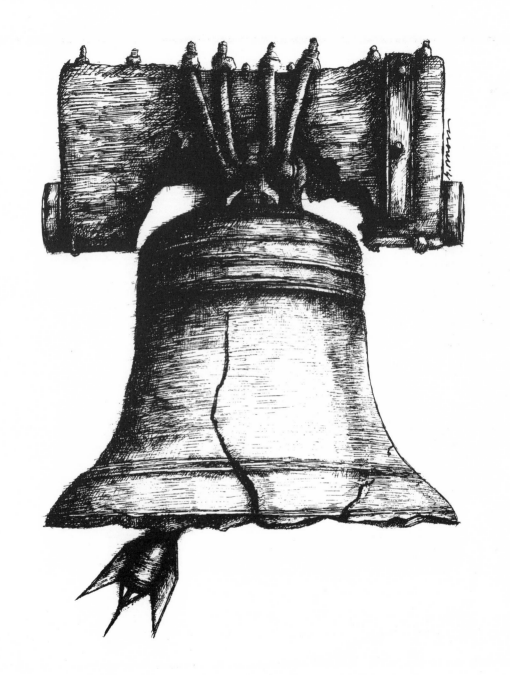

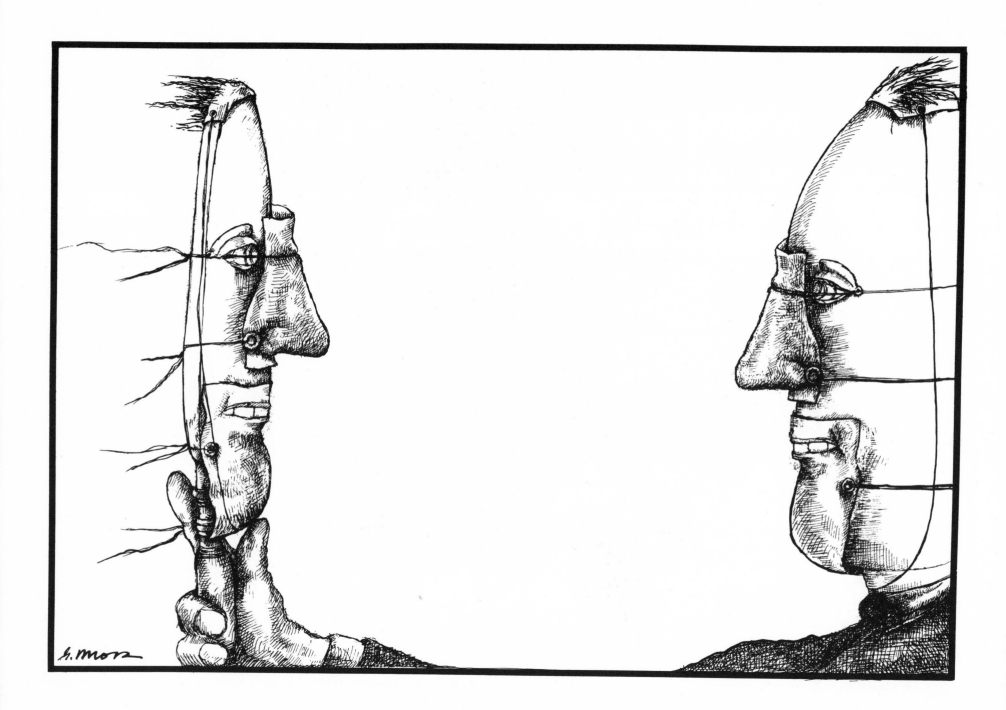

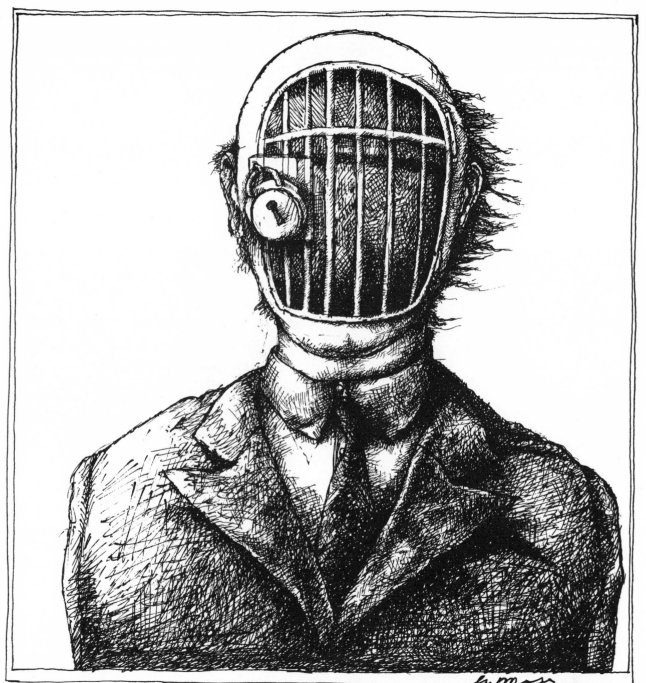

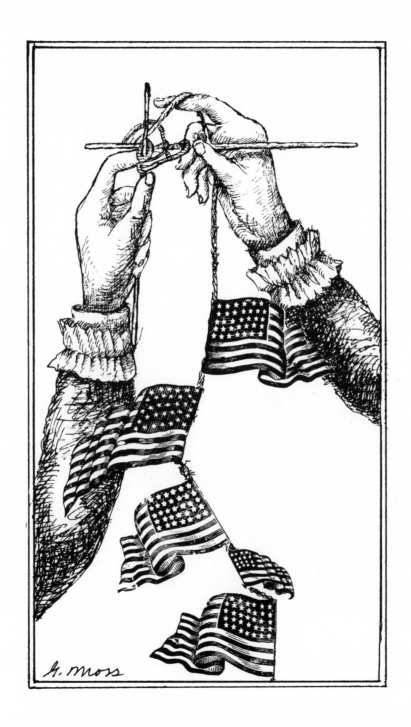

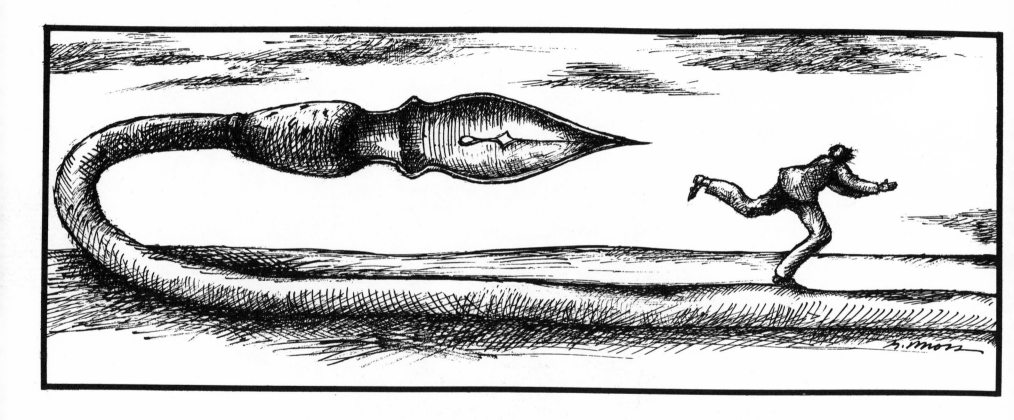

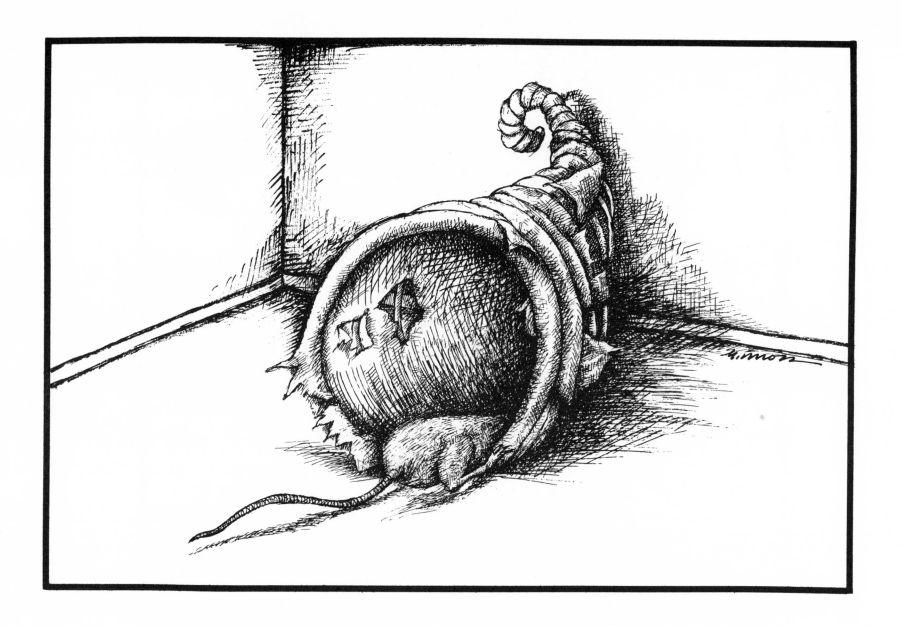

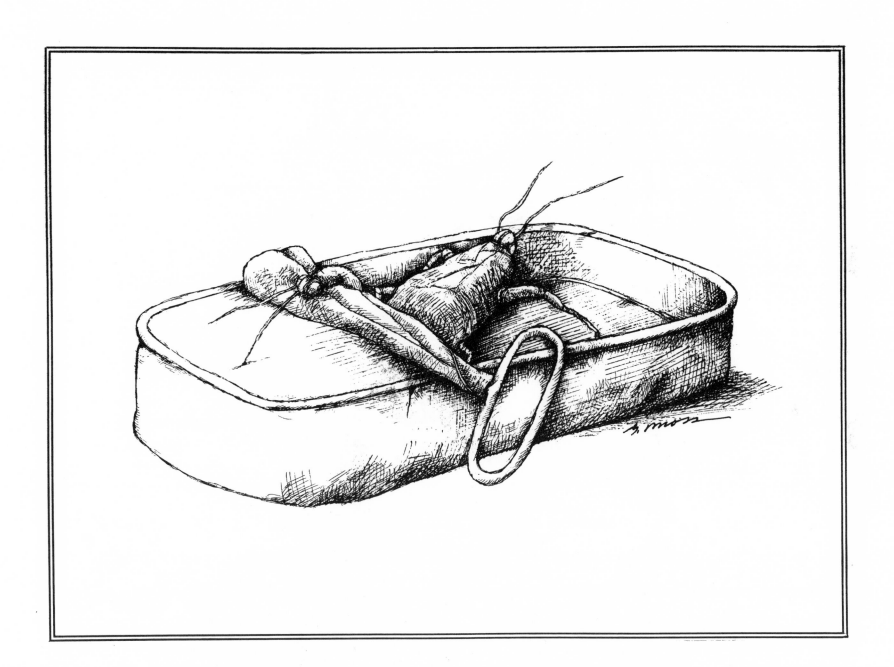

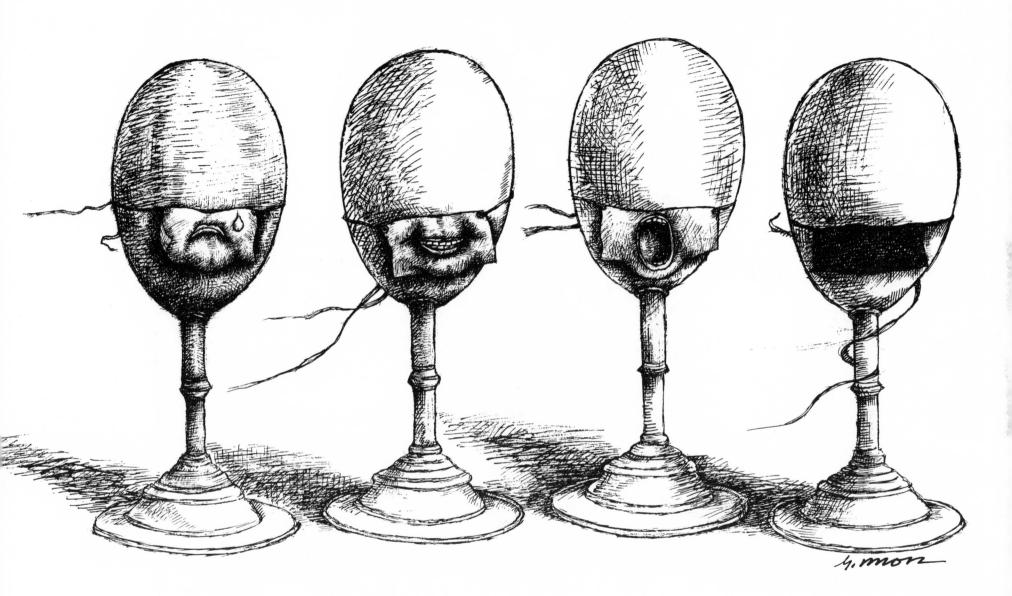

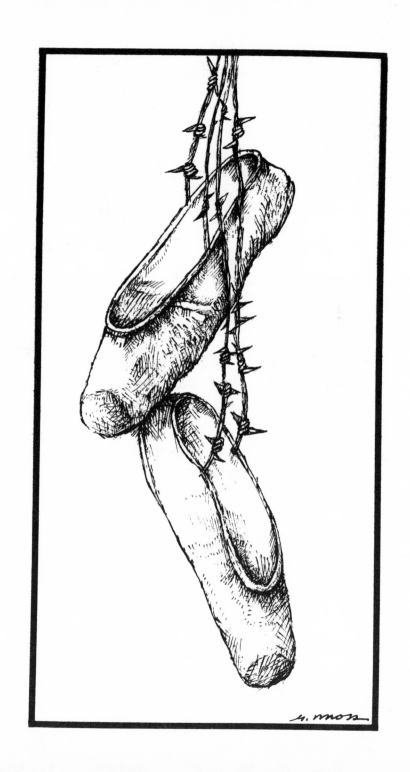

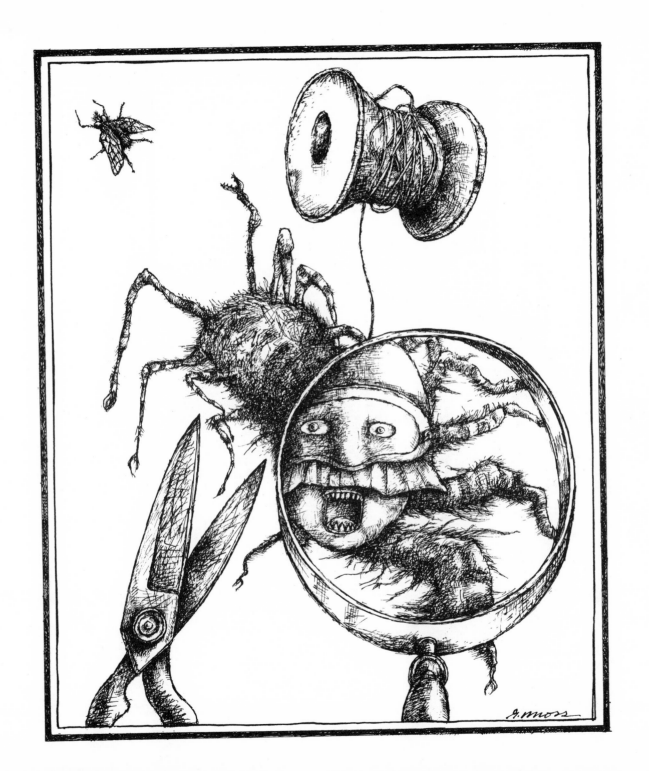

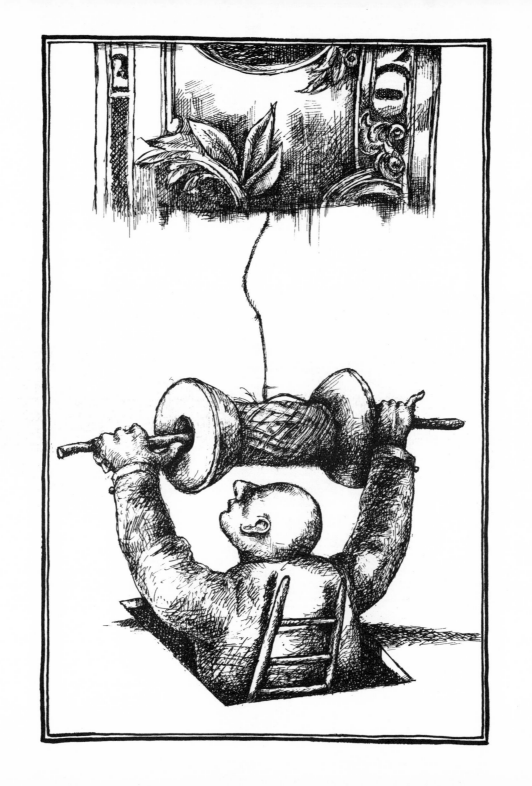

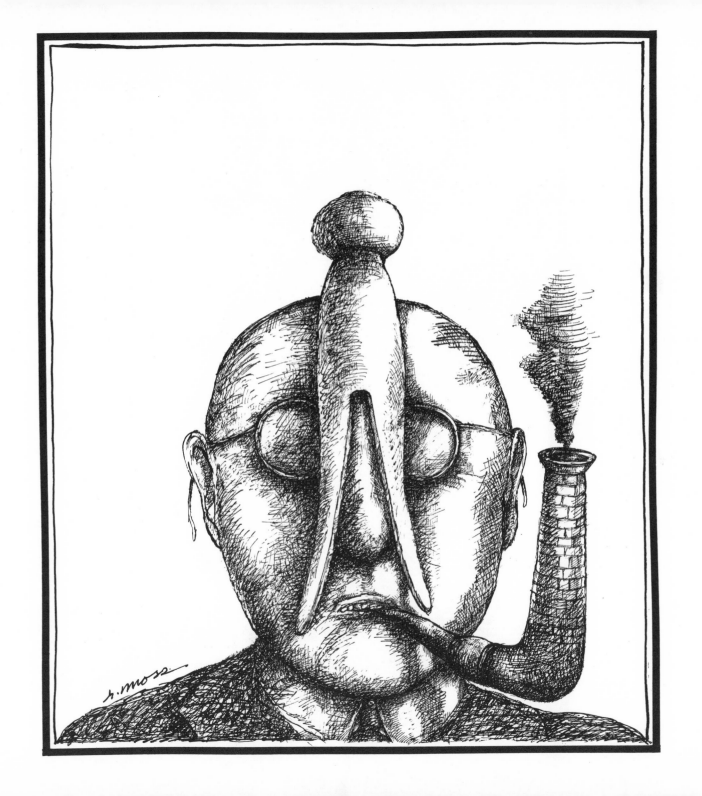

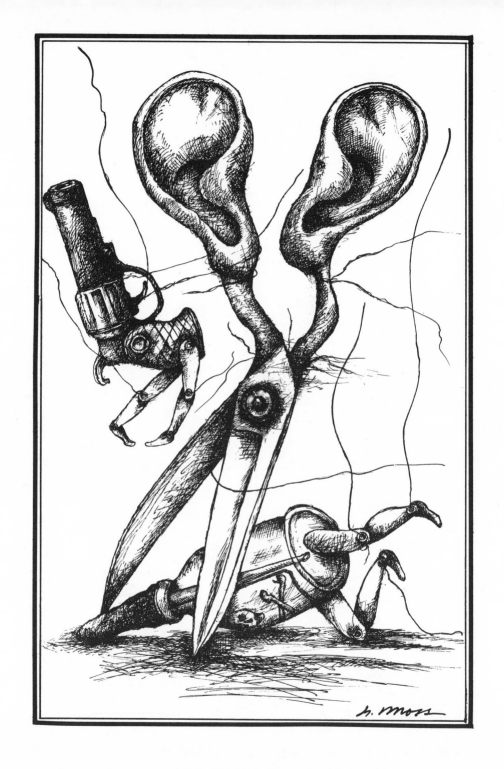

h. moss

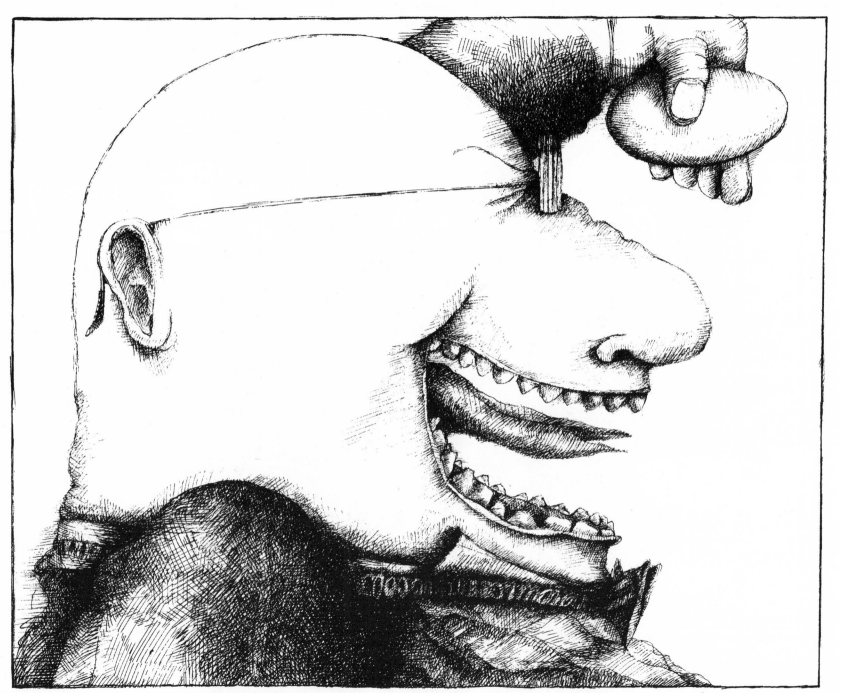

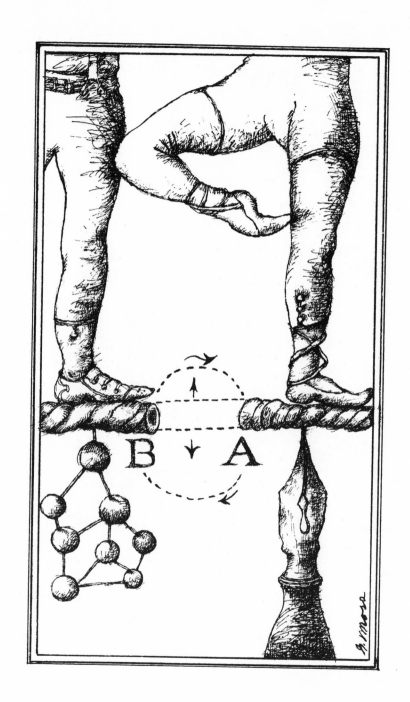

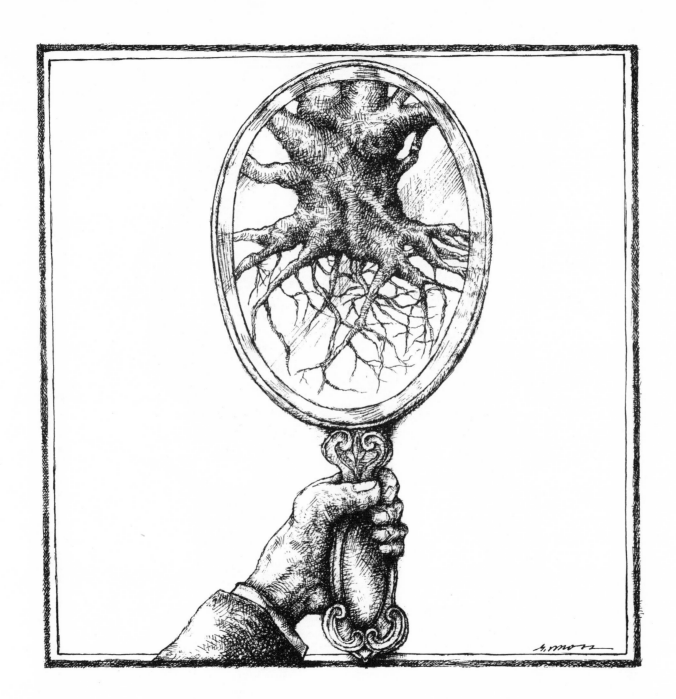